WARM

FUZZY

LOGIC

Dedication

To my wonderful wife, Marty, and my children; Sofia, Desiree', and Jacob; all of whom endure my learning curves of life, and still think I'm okay.

© 2015 Neil Brown All Rights Reserved

Introduction

Inside these pages you will find a very ***different*** and comprehensive explanation of the primary factors motivating mankind. You will learn how to better understand the underlying reasons why people behave as they do, how to deal with their behavior in a positive manner, and how to create win/win situations. This is not a book filled with motivational hype, but rather, an "outside the box" perspective on how to recognize and deal with underlying motivating factors.

You will learn about yourself: *why* you think the way you do, why you haven't changed or improved nearly as much as you would like, how to develop sufficient motivation to actually change or improve to the level you aspire, and why and how you should elevate your aspirations.

I know that sounds like a fairly heavy burden for me to impart, but you'll find it's not necessarily rocket science, and can be understood in more like wrist rocket terms.

This information will be presented in a clear, easily understood format with sufficient explanations within its own context for you to understand the material without the need of a dictionary. Though the pages are intended to be instructional, you will find this reads more like a conversation between you and me, rather than a manual. There will be instances in which I will assume your reaction, much in the same way as when you are asked to quickly add 1+9, 2+8, 3+7, 4+6, 5+5, then asked to name the first vegetable that comes to mind. The most common answer will be a carrot. Or, if you are asked to pick one of the following numbers:

1 2 3 4. You will most likely pick #3. Incidentally, the reason for adding the simple math before asking about the vegetable, is that it puts you in the frame of mind to answer questions quickly, which makes the response more accurate when you are asked what first comes to mind.

The contents of this book are intended for the general public, therefore technical jargon will be avoided when possible. Meanwhile, an attempt will be made to present the information in a way entertaining enough to keep you turning the pages (which aren't very many to begin with). There will be a few biblical references meant to illustrate the development of my personal moral character and view on Higher Powers. For the politically correct, you may substitute Higher Power when I refer to God. This is a book on motivation, not judgment; nor is it an attempt to proselytize.

Though the length of this book will be comparatively short, its impact will speak volumes, should you decide to implement even *some* of the information presented.

It is important that you keep an open mind while reading this book, because the hypothesis is relatively new, even in psychological circles. Only a handful of professionals have programs or treatments that even touch on the concepts you are about to unveil. Please understand that this is not a replacement for professional help, but rather a differing view to bring a new perspective that can be easily understood.

These unique concepts will show you how to empower yourself to seek solutions and not excuses. You will have at your fingertips a wealth of understanding of practical application that you won't find in any higher learning institution. This is not to say that what they teach is wrong; however, if you *had* been doing something wrong for 40 years, that only makes you an expert at doing something wrong. Again, please keep an open mind.

Knowledge is power… right? No, it's not! ***Wisdom*** is power. Knowledge is only a tool for wisdom to operate; otherwise, savants would rule the world. The more tools in your toolbox, however, the better prepared you are to make the right choices.

Value wisdom.

What is "Warm Fuzzy Logic?"

"Warm fuzzy logic" is the merging of *"warm fuzzies"* and *"fuzzy logic."* Before we delve into "warm fuzzy logic", let's first agree on a few definitions. First, what are "warm fuzzies"?

"*Warm fuzzies*" is a slang term that describes the feelings one gets from receiving love, acceptance, protection, material awards, and verbal or visual encouragement. They also result from self-confidence, self-talk resulting in self-esteem, and a feeling of contentment or importance. Each of these defining parts of warm fuzzies has a significant impact, and later I will go into detail on how each can be manipulated to become either healthy or abusive. You may have never thought that warm fuzzies could play a part in something with a negative context, but a little later, I'll show you how they can be harmful, and how to avoid the nonconstructive parts.

The other part of "warm fuzzy logic" is the "fuzzy logic" aspect. *"Fuzzy logic"* originated around 1965 by Lotfi Zadeh, a professor at the University of California at Berkley. He was using criteria based on simple rules, such as "IF X AND Y, THEN Z" in the development of computer theory.

An example of that in real life would be: If the room temperature is hot (X) and getting hotter (Y), then you should turn on the air conditioner (Z). Hot, in this case, is defined as a perception, not a degree of Fahrenheit or Celsius.

When you just now read that it was hot and getting hotter, you knew what to do to remedy the situation without my specifying what the actual temperature was.

Instead of being "absolutely true," or "absolutely false," *Fuzzy Logic* is an approach to computing based on degrees of truth.   Some truths may be more accurate than other truths, and *fuzzy logic* can be used in giving quick, simple and sufficiently valid solutions much in the same way the human mind assesses relevant truths.

So, how does computer science fit in with this book? Let's start with the relevant truths, such as the statement "She is beautiful."

That statement is normally followed by the evaluation using the old adage that "beauty is in the eye of the beholder." The perception of beauty would be true for some people, false for others, but in the mind of the beholder, it would be consistently considered accurate.

This is where the fusion of these phrases takes place: using *warm fuzzies* as the motivational criteria in evaluating the validity of how the *fuzzy logic* part makes enough sense for a determination to be made. This theory will not only reveal to you the motives of others, but it can also show you how to perceive and interpret your own motives.

In the Beginning

Let's start back at the beginning—as far back as you can remember—no, further: further than you can remember. Back to the day you were born, before you had cognitive reasoning. What was your main concern? It was the same as everyone else that was your age—YOURSELF. You had only one thing on your mind: *your* comfort. Though you didn't understand your own thoughts or demands, they were very consistent: feed me, hold me, talk to me, do whatever is necessary to make me feel comfortable and secure. There is absolutely nothing wrong with that. You were born that way. That's one program you've adhered to and one you'll *never* escape, and through this explanation, you'll see why.

Your needs were being met…food, shelter, emotional security. You became acutely aware if the food or shelter was missing, and you would let it be known quickly by a heartfelt, unequivocal cry that would usually immediately bring your guardian to your aid.

Not being aware of the need for emotional security, how did that come about? Through touch and sound at first. That's right, the cuddling and gentle dialogue you received as a baby were essential in your development. Just as a baby is born with the fear of falling or loud noises, he is also born with physical and emotional needs. They were needs that didn't need to be taught to you, but needs, nonetheless.

How did you express your needs? Yes, you were a little cry-baby. You were decidedly aware whenever you were in need, and you didn't mind letting people know about it. Whether it was obvious or not to you, *you* were number one. As you grew into a toddler, you found that there were things you wanted that you could not have. Your parents were probably grateful for your short attention span, and they would substitute something that was safer for you to have, or directing you to another adventure in which to focus. Sometimes your own curiosity could change your pursuit of the unavailable.

As you developed cognitive reasoning, you found that bartering could sometimes get you what you wanted. Sometimes you would have to give up lesser important things for what you determined to be more important. Though you might have to give up something whether tangible, behavioral, or in words, you were still in control, and that gave you a "warm fuzzy feeling".

You learned that certain behaviors produced certain results. This pattern that you went through time and again was absolute proof to you that there is a payoff for your behaviors. If there weren't, you would not have the motivation to follow through with them. You emotionally validated each behavior. Though you had to logically process how to go about getting what you wanted, the underlying and more important part was that you processed how you felt at the time, and compared it to what you sought to feel about any act before you executed it, always keeping in mind that your unwritten, unspoken goal is whatever is necessary to make you feel comfortable and secure, and if possible; special.

So how old are you at this point? It really doesn't matter, because neither you, nor I, nor anyone you or I know has ever passed this point. The *warm fuzzy* feeling you get from giving, from a job well done, from a compliment by a peer, from receiving a reward or award, social acceptance, the feeling of being loved, of being protected, all the feelings that make you feel important are (now, and in the future) what motivate you.

The way you deal with life is now inbred. It doesn't mean that you can't change how you deal with events with which you are confronted. But if you're going to change anything, it's good to understand that every thought or action you have or do is based upon how you will be personally affected. This can be a very good thing if you channel it correctly. In the following chapters, we will discuss when, how, why and which direction you may want to channel your thoughts and actions.

Warm Fuzzy Feelings

Let's dwell on that warm fuzzy feeling for a minute. What did it consist of? Well, that food and shelter part is now deeply ingrained in your feeling of security. So, it consists of being protected, loved, awarded for your behavior or input, a sense of control of your surroundings, and very important self-talk that you're someone of significance. These are motivators you are grounded in, and these compile your emotional needs.

Since you are a ball of emotions that thrives on warm fuzzy feelings, these warm fuzzies are what will motivate you for your entire life. If these needs are not met in appropriate ways, you will find ways to compensate. We'll touch on that a little later.

You might say "But what about love? I love my spouse, isn't that selfless?" The fact is that you admire and want to be around someone so much that you are willing to do what is necessary to nurture the feelings between you and your spouse is because it fosters the feelings *you* want to have. The same is for giving—it produces for you the warm fuzzies you want or hope to have, or you would not give. You've heard the phrase on many a telethon "Give until it hurts". You wouldn't give until it hurts unless you emotionally placed value on the pain. A little warm fuzzy for taking one for the team.

Granted, there are advantages to what people consider selfless giving. First, the warm fuzzies you receive from having given, and second, the benefit to the recipient for whatever it was that you gave. That's definitely a win/win situation, and a good target to shoot for.

Some of my Christian brethren will naturally say… Aha! You say, no such thing as selfless giving—what about Agape (the love of

God)? Excellent argument; and one of the best examples of a win/win situation. Remember, this is *warm fuzzy logic* and deals with perception. Here's how it fits into this theory. Basically, Christianity is based on one scripture; John 3:16 "For God so loved the world, that he gave his only begotten Son." (Why?) "That whosoever believeth in Him shall not perish, but have everlasting life." (Why everlasting life?) To be with Him. A warm fuzzy for God because he loves us and wants us to be with Him.

   Think about the sequence in the last passage. God loved first (emotional). Then he gave His son (action). The emotion caused the action. Not the other way around. The action did not cause the emotion. God may have even used logic to discern which was the best way to show his emotion, but the point here is that emotion incites action. Logic is merely a tool in emotionally deciding how to act.

In the next chapter, we will logically get emotional.

Logic vs. Emotion

You either will or will not believe that what I'm saying makes sense based on how you *logically* process this information, but you will apply or deny it based on how you *emotionally* process it. Can you emotionally convince yourself that this information fits your needs? If so, you will attempt to learn from it; otherwise, you'll just logically process it, and then emotionally blow it off. Either way the *decision* is emotional.

This is where many people have a big misconception about logic. You would think that as we grow older and seemingly become more logical, we say things like we admire someone who has "a good head on his shoulders." Meaning he seems to be more *driven* by logic.

Hogwash! Logic is merely a *tool* for emotion to ferret out options. Logic cannot be a *motivator* because it is not an emotion. Look at the root of these words:

Motivation: (Late Middle English: from Old French ***motif***, from late Latin ***motivus***, from ***mov***ere 'to move'.);

Em**ot**ion: (Middle French, from *emouvoir* to stir up, from Old French *esmovoir,* from Latin *emovēre* to remove) Motivation and emotion correlate with movement. This is where decisions for actions take place. People are not driven by logic, only emotion. A person that prides himself in his ability to think logically, probably doesn't realize that *pride* is the motivator to his logical thinking. If there were no emotional payoff, *logical* thinking wouldn't matter to him. I can't emphasize this enough! A hammer does not drive a nail. The *swing* of the hammer drives the nail! The hammer is only a tool.

If I *follow* a logical course of action, it's because I have first emotionally decided that it's the right or more important thing to do. I can even rationalize or alter my course of logic to fit my emotional agenda. So, what is my emotional agenda? It is an emotional pay-off that *I'm* seeking. Remember, I'm still number one.

If I give something to someone because I care about their welfare, that's especially good because they receive something that they didn't have to earn (warm fuzzy for them), and I get an emotional payoff of feeling good inside (warm fuzzy for me).

If you feel duty bound to do something, it is another way for you to tell yourself that you're important, that you're connected; part of the big picture. It's an emotional payoff.

Even the *thoughts* you entertain have an emotional payoff, or else you would substitute them for ones that did.

Did you ever love someone so much that you couldn't stop thinking about them? Warm fuzzies… emotional payoff.

Just Plain Logic

A quick exercise in logic vs. emotion. My computer follows instructions… it doesn't judge whether I am accidentally or intentionally feeding it correct or incorrect information. It doesn't judge whether I am smart enough to use it. It just reacts to input. It doesn't judge whether I am using it for good or bad purposes, personal or public gain. It doesn't matter to the computer what my religious preference is or even whether or not I'm wearing the wrong color tie.

It doesn't even get nervous when I cuss at it and tell it I'm going to replace it. Sometimes I think it really doesn't even like me. How can it always be so calm and complacent? It never passes judgment on me. Is it trying to be compassionate, or does it act that way because it just doesn't care? I don't know—it's just not human!
Stupid tool.

Your P.L.A.C.E. in Life

By now, you should understand that your place in life is taking care of number one. Your place in life is easy to remember as an acronym.

P. Protection
L. Love
A. Acknowledgement
C. Control
E. Esteem

Protection:

You need to feel like you are being protected from the elements. This involves a need for food and shelter. It also includes protection from violence. Out of this, you get a sense of security.

Love:

You need to feel like you are being loved, and that there is someone you can depend on to provide that for you. This does not have to be passionate or private. It can be passive. You just need to know that someone out there cares.

Acknowledgement:

When you attempt certain tasks, you need to feel like you are being acknowledged. You need to feel that you are contributing someway, somehow, and that you are a significant part of the team.

Control:

You need to maintain a sense of control over your environment. You need to be able to make decisions that will affect your life.

Esteem:

This pertains to self-esteem. Of course, others may contribute in building your self-esteem, but faith in yourself is an essential component in your place in life.

Each of these elements needs to be addressed, and whether you realize it or not, they are being addressed by you on a daily basis. They are the underlying criteria that are always taken into consideration, even if subconsciously, that makes up who you are. Everybody has the same needs that make up their P.L.A.C.E. in life, and it would serve you well to acknowledge that the people you come in contact with also have their P.L.A.C.E. that they are trying to deal with. The circumstances that they encounter while doing so, are different from yours and can easily affect them differently.

The achievement of warm fuzzies for all is a good goal and keeps people from seeking less favorable ways of fulfilling the needs that they have to maintain their P.L.A.C.E. in life.

Sometimes I have the opportunity to talk to people one-on-one about their place in life and what goals they have. As an emotional reference for them to remember, I have them point to each finger as I go through the explanation of each letter of the acronym of life's necessities, and once we're finished with the fifth finger, I slowly close the fingers into a fist and gently press their fist to their heart as I point out that it's in their hands as to how they are going to deal with their "place in life".

    I often ask them to picture themselves five or ten years from now, and tell me if they see that things are different. They always say yes. Again, as an emotional reference to add impact to my message, I gently shake my head, as if to say no, and look them squarely in the eye and say; "The only differences you'll see that will materialize in the future are the differences you make happen today."

Goals are great to have, but unless there is emotional conviction behind them, you won't experience them.

I don't know of anyone that can tell me what 'pie in the sky' actually tastes like.

Negative Emotions

When I talked about the necessities of your place in life, I was referring to requirements, not options. Those needs will get met one way or another. Revenge, hate, guilt, misbehavior and self-degradation are the result or compensation for being deprived of the necessities. You *will* try to control your thoughts or your environment, even if you have to distort the logic to make it happen. Each part of the P. L. A. C. E. in your life has a positive or negative direction it can take.

The self-talk of "I deserve this abuse"; "I have to be the martyr"; "what they don't know won't hurt them"; "they had it coming" all boils down to compensation or retribution for bad experiences. Yes, you do get warm fuzzies from these also. Many times, you'll find you get comfortable in your fox hole. That way, you stay in control. After all, you still have to take care of number one, and if 'they' won't help, you'll do it alone.

I sometimes find myself struggling with the scenario of not attempting to accomplish something just so I can reserve the right to hold on to the warm fuzzy wherein I tell myself "sure,

I could have done it if I would have given it my all".

So how do we change from any or all of this negativity? That depends. Do you really want to? Remember this, *you only do what is important to you*, so you have to decide that it's more important to get out of the rut you're in, rather than languish in the mire. You have to stop consoling your own grief. That just makes it worse. It creates a self-fulfilling prophecy.

A very good way for many people to begin an effective, long-lasting change is to have some type of turning point. To some people, that requires allowing their circumstances to become so unbearable, that they feel they have no *choice* but to change if they want to get out of their predicament. That's a hard place to go for a pivot point, and not someplace one would choose to go, but, because it's so emotional to them, it has a profound effect. Usually, people having a turning point to that degree make substantial changes in their surroundings or circumstances.

They inherently understand; *that with which you surround yourself is what you become.* If you want to be kind, surround yourself with people you believe to be kind. Spend more time with the people whose attributes you yourself would like to emulate. You will only reap from the field you sow. Make sure you're on good ground.

Change doesn't have to be dramatic, but for it to be effective, it does have to be emotional.

I was told a story about a person who was interviewing several rich men because he was trying to find the secret to wealth. He couldn't find anyone who could give him a firm cut and dry answer. He finally came upon a wealthy man who did have an answer for him. The interview was being held in the rich man's house in a large room with large glass doors that overlooked an extravagant pool. The interviewer asked, "What must I do to be wealthy?" The rich man said, "I'll not only tell you how to become wealthy, I'll show you." The interviewer thought to himself, "This is great! He's actually going to show me the secret of how to become wealthy!"

The rich man said come with me. They went out through the glass door and the rich man walked right into the pool up to his waist, motioning to the interviewer to follow him in. The interviewer thought this a bit out of the ordinary, but he followed him into the pool anyway. The rich man said, "This is where I'm going to show you how to be wealthy." With that, the rich man put the interviewer's head under water and held him there. The interviewer thought, "This is strange. I asked him how to become wealthy, and he puts my head under water." A few moments go by with no change, and the interviewer is still being held under water. Thinking it's time to come up for a breath, the interviewer tries to lift his head up, but the rich man continues to hold him down. He tries harder to get up, but the rich man holds him down more firmly. He struggles to get up, but the more he struggles, the more he is held down. Finally, with all he can muster, he tries one last forceful burst and frees himself, and immediately takes several gasping breaths. He turns to the rich man and said, "Why did you do that? All I wanted to do was to find how to become wealthy." The rich man responded with, "When you want to be wealthy as much as you wanted to take your next breath, you'll *be* wealthy." The rich man knew the value of emotional impact. Just telling him would have little effect, and the interviewer would have kept seeking the answer not knowing how to value real determination.

What do you want? If you're going to logically determine what it is that you want, you'll need to decide if you have the emotional backing to actually make the decision, because the decision itself won't be a decision unless you emotionally decide to follow through with whatever it takes to get you where you want to go. If you don't process this emotionally, it is mere fodder for contemplation, and will go nowhere. If you do decide to change, make it visible and measurable to add validation to the warm fuzzies you seek.

What's the Agenda?

Okay, now that I know my P. L. A. C. E. in life, should I have an agenda? Do I already have an agenda? What *is* my agenda? What *was* my agenda? What *will always be* my agenda?

My agenda is what is important to me. Will my agenda ever change? No,
I *only* do what is important to me.
If that sounds a little self-centered, it is. And guess what, so are you. Let me show you why

that's not a bad thing. If it's important to me to show people that I have a giving nature—I give. If it's important to me to let my wife know I love her, I do what's necessary to make sure she knows it. If it's important to me to accomplish a goal, I accomplish it. If it's *not* important for me to accomplish a goal, I say I did my best. Why do I say I did my best when I really didn't?

Because, just like everybody else, it's important to me to feel good about myself, so I lie rather than admit I took on a task that wasn't really important enough for me to do what was necessary to accomplish it.

When I asked my children to do something, and later on, when I found out it wasn't done, I would ask why. The response used to be "I forgot." I asked why they forgot, and they would say "What do you mean 'why'?
I just forgot! I'm only human!"
I would reply with "Of course you're human! That's why I know there's a reason why you forgot. It's because it wasn't *important* enough for you to remember."

Even memory can be a matter of convenience according to your agenda.

I was pleasantly surprised one day when I had asked my oldest daughter about an errand she had promised to run, but didn't. When I asked if she had done it, her answer was, "I'm sorry, I didn't make it important enough for me to remember."

I smiled and thanked her for her honesty. A warm fuzzy for me, because I felt I was getting through, and also one for her because she took pleasure in knowing what my reaction would be.

Once you know that you're doing (or not doing) things based on their importance to you, it's easier to understand why people strive for, or put off doing certain things. What's important to you *is* what motivates you.

You may start to categorize people by their actions... honest people do honest things, dishonest people do dishonest things, good people do good things, and desperate people do desperate things, etc. The temporary drawback with just using this categorical line of reasoning is that people's motivating factors can change. Usually when someone changes, there's some type of turning point that either "knocks some sense into" or embitters people to change how they act. Nevertheless, their agenda will filter back into being the same. You'll find them doing what's important to them.

Where Did the Time Go?

I have so many things I want to do, but I just don't have time for them. It seems nobody has time to enjoy or do the good things in life. You have something important to do, but don't have time to spend working on it.

All three of the previous statements are contradictions within themselves. To understand this, you need to view time as a matter of importance. No, I don't just mean that time is important; I mean 'what is important to you' is what you *will* spend your time on. Time is a *function* of importance. The placement of time on any given subject will be determined by the genuine importance of that subject.

There will be times I find myself doing something that will lead to nothing because I just like stuffing things into my nothing box, because I am comfortable with my very own private little box. Surprisingly, every time I look for results in my favorite little box, nothing is there. Sometimes I get so busy stuffing things into my nothing box that I don't have time for things that I know should be important to me, but I shudder to think of giving it up. Some people, even my wife, label that as 'procrastination'. What an evil name for such a cute little box.

I'm pretty sure that the reason they use the word potato in the phrase "couch potato" is because there's so much time spent in a vegetative state. The sad thing (for me) is that I need to de-value the nothing box, which is so important to me. If I don't stop stuffing it so frequently, my question will eventually change from:

"I have so much to do…Where did the time go?"
 to:
"I had so much I wanted to do…Where did my life go?"

Get Over

One day one of my employees and I were talking about motivation. He explained to me what he considered to be his theory of life. It was what I call the "Get Over" theory. It was all based on manipulating the circumstances and or your fellow man, so you could get over on them, as in "pull one over", "pull the wool over", "get one over on someone". Basically, one-upmanship.

He felt you weren't in control unless you controlled the outcome of whatever you were doing no matter how you had to manipulate the circumstances, or the people involved. Of course, there were hypothetical limits like not breaking the law, but it didn't exclude bending it to a large extent.

It bothered me, the thought of someone seeking ways to get what they want without concern for the values of the other people they're encountering. I told him I couldn't see this resulting in anything other than a predatory nature. He agreed about the predatory assumption with the reply "People *are* predatory by nature, and you have to look out for yourself". This conversation was a little unsettling to me as he seemed to be a good-natured, likable person. I was kind of hoping he didn't really believe this, and he might be just regurgitating conversations he had heard over a few beers.

I talked to him further about creating win/win situations and considering whether the effect on others, as well as the personal outcome, should be taken into consideration before making a decision to proceed. He said that if it turns out to be a win/win, then that's a matter of happenstance, and that's cool too, but that would not be the primary goal. I was beginning to see that his fear was, that if you gave up your pursuit of "getting over", you would be the victim of someone trying to "get over on you".

I didn't get to work with him for very long because after his shift one day he loaded a to-go box to the brim with very expensive food, and was about to walk out the back door with his jacket on as I was coming in the same door. He knew it was an adamant policy of mine not to allow employees to take food off the premises. We inspected the contents of the box, and I had him put the food down before he left. The next day when he showed up for work, I told him that I couldn't allow him to "get over on me" this time because there were witnesses who saw what he was trying to get away with, and I had no choice but to let him go, or I would lose the honor and respect of the employees who were willing to follow the rules.

This is where one of the needs in your "place in life" comes into play. As I mentioned earlier in the book about getting your needs met, you will attempt to accomplish getting them met, whether through proper or abusive means. Control is a need. I'm sure he was getting warm fuzzies from considering himself a victor when he did get over on other people. In this instance he *was* getting his control needs met, but in a psychologically unhealthy manner. To this day, it saddens me that I had to take those measures, but I believed I had to maintain the integrity of the business for the sake of the other employees.

To see if your "control" need is in check, ask yourself before you act whether you will feel that when it's done, that you have acted with integrity, and will you feel that you have made an honorable decision.

Empowerment vs. Manipulation

Are empowerment and manipulation really different? Where do you draw the line? In a nutshell, manipulation has a negative connotation and is usually considered persuading someone for personal gain through inappropriate means.

Empowerment, however, has a more positive feel to it and involves appropriate means, but still, they both cause someone to think or act based on your input.

Manipulation can be as blatant as lying to someone face-to-face or as subtle as allowing someone to be persuaded by intentionally omitting a seemingly insignificant detail. Some people label this as passive/aggressive.

Empowerment, as honorable as it may seem, may still involve omitting a few possibly insignificant details.

Is manipulation a way to bias an otherwise unbiased view of options, or would it qualify as empowerment under the category of honorable intentions?

The deciding factor should be whether it is directed toward the well-being of the recipient, and not necessarily the administrator.

So, do you need to consider whether the "ends justify the means?" The moral absolutionist will tell you to never consider grey areas. Follow along with me for a moment. There were times as an employer I would make attempts of creating win/win scenarios, like when I would intentionally leave something not quite finished or out of place and stand back at a distance to watch to see if one of my employees would follow up and complete the job without being asked. My intention was to catch them in the act of doing something right, and I would promptly commend them for their going the extra mile, which would generate warm fuzzies for both of us. Is that manipulation or empowerment? It could be manipulation if you look at it as though I tricked someone into doing something because I wasn't going to wait around just hoping to catch them in the act. You could look at it as empowerment because of the warm fuzzies I was able to create for someone from a situation of my own making.

What if I told them after it was over, exactly why I set up the scenario? Wouldn't that be a blow to their ego? They would definitely feel used and abused. That would lead them to believe that they were incapable of going the extra mile by themselves, and had to be prodded. If I *had* told them my intentions, then I, on the other hand, would have been one hundred percent up front and honest, like everyone says you're supposed to be, but it would be at their emotional expense. Well, I personally think I would rather have them learn from examples of how I treat people, and let the results determine whether my intentions are to manipulate or empower.

Basically, manipulation focuses on outcomes that benefit the manipulator, and empowerment focuses on outcomes that benefit the manipulated. If there were no flawed individuals in need of redemption, we'd have no need to consider grey areas, and could always join in with the moral absolutionists. In any event, your primary goal *should* be to find ways to achieve honorable results through honorable means, and you won't have many grey areas to consider.

Prejudice

So, is the definition of prejudice simply pre-judging someone or something? Depending on which dictionary you search, it is almost always defined as a feeling or opinion which is usually referred to as negative. If you look it up at dictionary.com, the first definition is… "an unfavorable opinion or feeling formed beforehand or without knowledge, thought, or reason". Wait a minute. Is that even possible? To form an unfavorable opinion without knowledge, thought or reason?

Homie don't think so.

Did you just form an opinion as you read that last sentence? Do you know enough about me to assign a prejudgment about my use of the word homie? Did that infer an ethnic background or an association with certain people who routinely use that word?

Okay, so we need to back up on this one a little bit. If we can redefine the word prejudice to mean judgment based on *information at hand*, then we might be able to see a new perspective and delve into motivations a little.

Let me use an example. Let's say that I, as a child, walked home from school every day, and three houses down from my home there was a big vicious dog that barked fiercely at me every time I went by. Since I knew he was behind a fence, he couldn't get to me. I might have teased him with a stick now and then just to show him I wasn't intimidated. I've judged from past experiences that I was safe. I pre-judged that I would be safe every day. One day, as I was teasing him, he found a weak spot in the bottom of the fence. I could see that he was climbing out and he was going to attack me. I ran as fast as I could and barely got inside the door of my house as he jumped at the door which slammed as he crashed against it. Quite a harrowing

experience, but aside from that, what had just changed? The weak spot was always there, just never attempted. I could no longer pre-judge that I would be safe. I may have even gone around the block on the way home for a while. Had I known then about the weak spot, I may have had some prejudice in considering a fear of being attacked when determining which route I would take. Did I just change my prejudices based on my experiences?
Yup.

It doesn't matter whether you call it prejudice or not, either way, my behavior as well as my thought pattern changed as a result of outside input. That's the part that matters. The information I *now have at hand* helps direct my thoughts and actions, and in that case, toward self-preservation or protection.

Okay, so where do you go with this? It's simple; prejudices are decisions, thoughts or actions based on current available information, and people don't go beyond what they're taught.

You're probably wondering why I threw in that part about people not going beyond what they're taught. If no one teaches you about other possibilities, you tend to stay with what you know, and make decisions based on current information. After all, we are creatures of habit.

You can be taught through instruction, outside influences, and research. Research is a pattern developed through instruction. Let me expound on that. You might argue that you had learned how to tie your shoes without instruction or outside influence. Nope! Someone taught you how to research your thoughts and think through the possibilities of how to make it work. That's why it's important to teach children how to think for themselves to learn how to solve problems, rather than just having them learn by following orders. Allow them to search and research.

"Think outside your limits." I didn't want to keep using the cliché "think outside the box" because clichés put me back *in* the box.

If I were trampled by unicorns every time I went near them, I would tend to have a prejudice against unicorns. If I never met a unicorn, but was told that I would be trampled by them every time I encountered one, I would probably avoid them by virtue of my accepted prejudices of unicorns. And yes, I did say virtue. Prejudices can protect you as well as cause harm. Why use unicorns to illustrate a point? To show I can also have prejudices for the nonexistent.

In determining others' motivations, as well as your own, you need to take into consideration what dialogues and decisions are being encountered as a result of the person's information at hand.

Who Owns My Thoughts?

Did you ever have an argument that was so bothersome to you that when it was over you still thought about it? You thought about it later that day. You thought about it that evening. You thought about it when you went to bed. You woke up in the middle of the night thinking about it. You couldn't get back to sleep because you kept thinking about it. Once you did get back to sleep it was the first thing you thought of in the morning.

The person that you had the argument with probably forgot about your argument, or went on along his merry way not being bothered by it at all. How is it that particular person gets to live in *your* head rent free? It's almost as if he controls the frequency and severity of how often you return to those thoughts.

It's because you've *given* control to him. He didn't steal it, and probably doesn't even know he has control, but obviously he has it and you don't.

So why do you allow him to have control and not you? It could be that you don't realize that this is damaging to your psyche. It could be that you don't realize that he *has* control, even though you are showing signs and symptoms of having relinquished it to him. It could be that you don't know how to regain control.

I am not saying that people shouldn't have influence on you or your thoughts. That cannot be avoided. As a matter of fact, every word or action will have an effect on you, though it may be in the slightest way, it still does affect you. Often, you'll hear people being referred to as being a product of their environment. It may be true, but it doesn't necessarily infer that this would even be a bad thing. You'll want to recognize it in the realm of *influence* which will help you to stay away from being dominated and not merely influenced.

You need to realize that only *you* can assign ownership to what you think. If someone else has ownership, it's because you've allowed it to happen. Take time once in a while to think about what is or was happening and why. It's a good habit to get into, especially when you begin to feel flustered. Rethink your situation. Ask yourself "Why do I feel this way?" A lot of times it's a needless remnant thought that you haven't released because you've given it too much value.

Did you ever say something that you regretted and wanted to take back and just erase it from your memory? Can you actually do that? I often tell the story of a man who was working in his garage with his six-year-old standing by, who was watching him intently and asked if he could participate. The dad said sure, and got a piece of two-by-four and a small nail and handed the child the hammer. The son did a good job of starting the nail, and with several hits of the hammer, the nail was starting to go in. Then the dad said "Okay, now take the nail out." The child worked diligently on the nail, and finally got it out. The dad then said "Good, now, the most important part; take the hole out." The boy looked confused, and, though he was proud that he could figure out how to get rid of the nail, his pride was diminishing because he couldn't figure out what, according to his dad, was the most important part, which was how to get rid of the hole. He looked at his dad almost in tears, and said "Dad, I can't take the hole out." His dad said, "You're right son, that's the most important part, and this is the reason why it's so important...

"You know that when you say something mean to someone or call them names, that hurts them, right?" "Yes" was the reply. "That's like hammering a nail into them. Words can also hurt people too." The child nodded. "You can say you're sorry, and that's like taking the nail out right?" Another nod. "But you can't take out the hole, and that's what people remember even after you said you're sorry. They remember that you said you're sorry, but they still remember the hole. They remember that they felt bad because of what was said. If we don't say mean things, we don't have to worry about taking out any holes."

Think back about someone you've forgiven... No, really, stop what you're doing right now and take five or ten seconds and think about it. Whether they said they were sorry or not, you just remembered that there was emotional pain. Did you just prove the point of 'forgive but not forget'? To forgive and forget is a rarity. Play it on the safe side.

It may take some time to getting used to thinking about your effect on people before you speak because sometimes it seems like life is a bullet train. But unless you take the time to assess what's on the map, you'll be going nowhere, though you'll certainly get there fast.

Authority

Where does authority come from? Who has it? Who deserves it? What is the best way to deal with it?

Authority comes in many forms. Written, acclaimed, transferred, usurped, inferred, inherent, perceived, and yes, even earned. I see no need to go into all aspects of its origin to get to the points I want to cover. As I see it, the most important part is how to deal with it from both the disciplinarian and the disciplined side.

From the disciplined side, authority is a measure of honor you bestow upon someone who you perceive to have the responsibility to act in a supervisory position. If someone has authority over you, it is your responsibility to honor the position they hold. As I mentioned in the last chapter about thought ownership, you are not obligated to let them control your thoughts. Just remember as a part of being an honorable person, you, as one under authority must honor the position assigned to those who have authority over you, whether you agree or not.

There have been many a time I have disagreed with someone who has had authority over me, but I succumbed to their dictates in honor of their position. How do I do that without becoming resentful? My self-talk would be that I am serving the Lord who is the ultimate master and for whom I work; therefore, I can feel comfortable that I'll be rewarded for my efforts. If not from the theological standpoint, you could tell yourself that you are a principled person who respects authority and you are vindicated by standing on your principles. Be aware though, that sometimes standing on your principles may mean removing yourself from the circumstances. If you are expected to lie, cheat or steal, you may be put in a position where you have to discern whether you value your principles more than the current state of affairs. You need to consider what is most beneficial for you and whether it will supply the warm fuzzies you can be proud of.

From the disciplinarian side, authority is not just a position you hold over others, it is a responsibility to direct and maintain oversight to achieve the goals that either you or *your* authority figure set while preserving the well-being of those under your authority. As the great pseudo-philosopher Bob Dylan said, "You gotta serve somebody".

If you have the mindset that you will be held accountable for the actions of those under your authority, you will be more closely concerned with getting things accomplished through your subordinates that will justify the respect that they convey.

When you are in a position of authority, the more concern you show for your subordinates, the more likely they are to respect you not only for your position, but as a person. A little-known fact is that you are more effective when you are respected as a person who cares about the people involved, more than the position you hold. That being said, you shouldn't let your authority be diminished by lowering your standards so as to allow people under you to skate. That actually lessens your effectiveness as well as the value of your authority. Your job is to bring them up to your standards.

One note for the "man of the house"… I know in scripture the man is the head of the household as Christ is the head of the church. Wives are directed to submit to the authority of the husband. This doesn't make the man the master and the wife the slave. Remember, Christ gave his life for the love of the church. For this passage to work, the man has to love and care for the wife as he would his own body. This takes dedication to helping her become the best she can be. Feel her pain, rejoice in her happiness as if it were your own. Treat her as a gift from God, and you'll get the respect and consideration you deserve.

Co-dependence vs. Compassion

Where does co-dependence differ from compassion? When does sharing another person's burden become too burdensome? When does helping someone else hurt you? Are you to desire less to feel you have more? Is there a cut-and-dry answer as to how much of our brother's keeper we need to be? NO, only guidelines.

One of the highest impact of warm fuzzies is a win/win situation. Higher still, is the win/win which is not transactional, but an act of compassion or benevolence. The warm fuzzies you get from compassionate acts provides the self-esteem and assurance of self-worth so vital to keep your P.L.A.C.E. in balance.

Remember the old proverb "feed a man a fish and you've fed him for a day—teach him to fish, and you've fed him for a lifetime". When you help a person work through his problems instead of fixing them for him, you assist in building the foundation for him to work through his own problems. Once he has confidence in himself, like you, he will seek to solve his own problems, and possibly even share his knowledge.

To assist your well-being and to become a better person, you should surround yourself with good people because they will influence you to your benefit.
Sometimes, however, for *your* benefit, you may need to be one of those people *doing* the surrounding.

Forgive Who?

One of the most profound psychological experiences I've encountered took me by surprise, of course, because it had such an emotional impact on me. It was when I was watching a sermon on TV where a pastor was talking about forgiveness and the bitter relationship he had with his father. He was going on and on about how his father mistreated him and the bad deeds that the pastor was exposed to, along with the countless arguments and disagreements on points that neither he nor his father would bend, let alone succumb to.

At one point, after being bothered by the teachings in the bible that related to "forgiving one another as you have been forgiven", and after several prayers on the matter, this pastor decided he was going to confront his father and forgive him, so as to put himself in closer fellowship with his heavenly father. So, during the confrontation I fully expected to hear the pastor say that he wanted to reconcile with God, and in order to do that, that he would express his forgiveness to his earthly father, saying that he forgave his father for all the mean treatment and pain that his father had caused him over so many years.

Well, that didn't happen.

Instead, the pastor said to his father; "Dad, I came to ask you to forgive me for the bitterness and resentment that I have felt for you all these years. I've carried these feelings for so long, that it causes heart-ache when I think about all the times I could have spent relishing the memories of the good times we did have, but I allowed them to be overshadowed by the greed for my own self-righteousness. My own pride prevented me from seeking a good relationship with you and I am truly sorry; will you please forgive me?"

His father embraced him, forgave him, and said "Son, I am so sorry. I had no idea that you felt that way, could you forgive me for all the bad things that I've done to you?" The pastor also forgave him and now their relationship has been reconciled.

That goes completely against the teachings of the modern-day concept of forgiveness. It always seems to be that for anyone to forgive, it has to be me (that's in power), has chosen to forgive you (the recipient of my righteousness) in order for me to be in congruency with an even higher power (which is God).

As universal a practice as that may seem, it doesn't quite fit in with the biblical references of humility to gain favor with the Lord. Try as you might, it's nearly impossible to have contempt for someone whose forgiveness you feel you need to seek. This theory seems to want to veer away from the "It's all about me" concept and puts it in an "All about someone else" category. Or does it? If this were you…
Did you feel you did the right thing?

You got a Warm fuzzy.

Did it show you're not so self-righteous?

...Warm fuzzy.

Did it take a burden off your chest?

...Warm fuzzy.

Did it release further resentment?

...Warm fuzzy again.

Though you can't escape the warm fuzzy logic, it does show that the warm fuzzies you get become exponential when you're *not* focused on yourself. And guess what? It doesn't just work on forgiveness. The point of this chapter is to illustrate my personal insight on the value of seeking a higher power to reconcile with simply because…

It's easier to forgive once you've been forgiven.

Giving Without

Why is it that I don't feel generous when tax time rolls around? I'm giving. Giving a lot. Giving is a good thing, right? Why then is the only time I feel good about any part of tax time is when it's finally over…unless I get audited, and then it's not over.

It's because I'm not really giving. It's confiscation. They'll get it sooner or later. It's been said the only two things you have to do in life is die and pay taxes. Not true. You can go to jail if you refuse to pay taxes. Few, if any people consider the "Render unto Caesar" thing a charitable act, and for good cause.

Okay, then what about when I give my time and money to a worthy cause or needy person and never get anything in return? Sometimes, not even a "Thank you." Same problem. It's not giving. It is bartering, where you put your investment up front with an expectation of some type of return, whether it is something tangible or simply a kind word, it is a ***transaction***.

There's a big misconception about giving. Giving is not giving unless it's motivated by love. In this sense, good will is a form of love. True giving is giving a gift (tangible or intangible) with hopes that it will benefit the receiver. You can't *really* give without loving, nor can you love without giving. If you love someone, you *do* something about it.

Depending on whether you're referring to the noun or the verb; love (the noun) is an emotional attachment you have for someone or something. In this context, we're talking about the verb, love, not the noun. How is it manifested? By your actions. Love is an action. How do you place a value on love but by action? The only time you see love without giving is "tough love". Or is it? Isn't tough love an act of giving that just doesn't coincide with the recipient's expectations? When I gave my children a spanking, it was because I loved them and wanted them to grow up to be good honorable people.

When you refer to someone as a loving person, does that mean that they think about love all the time, or that they show it by way of their actions? Obviously, you shall know them by their fruits.

Okay, so where do the warm fuzzies fit in?

You can get warm fuzzies by making a transaction that benefits you.

You can get warm fuzzies from making a transaction that benefits both you and the other party.

And, you can get them from just giving or doing something to someone for their sole benefit.

All three are examples of warm fuzzies, but in sequential order of how much they contribute to *your* wellbeing. You'll find that not only is the latter exponentially more satisfying, but stays longer in your memory and leads to the desire to repeat.

If you take the *miser* out of *miser*able, that leaves you able.

I See Silver

As you have probably guessed from earlier chapters, at one time I was the owner and operator of a local restaurant. I had thirty employees and was doing fine. In our town we have snowbirds; those wonderful elderly people that come south for the winter to enjoy our banter and fare. Well, the time had come for them to leave as spring was approaching.

We usually had hard times during the summer due to seasonal sales volumes, and sometimes I had to use saved past profits to accommodate bills in light of the diminishing sales throughout the summer. This time I was experiencing an especially difficult time because of newer restaurants in the outskirts of my local clientele. Bills were piling up, and one of my greatest fears was not making payroll. Unpaid utilities etc. would shut us down, so I definitely had to pay them, but I couldn't bear the thought of unpaid employees. Stress was a major player in those days. It looked like I would have to close the business before the next season could arrive. Sometimes I would go back in my office and nearly weep at the thought of disappointing people who looked up to me and counted on me for their survival. During one of those painful sole searching moments I looked for a diversion to my sorrow and checked my email. I don't know who sent it, but it changed my perspective when I needed it most.

This is the story.

It was a story about a lady that was in a Bible study group that had a lesson on

Malachi 3:3 "He will sit as a refiner and purifier of silver."

This verse puzzled some women in a Bible study and they wondered what this statement meant about the character and nature of God.

One of the women offered to find out the process of refining silver and get back to the group at their next Bible Study.

That week, the woman called a silversmith and made an appointment to watch him at work. She didn't mention anything about the reason for her interest beyond her curiosity about the process of refining silver. As she watched the silversmith, he held a piece of silver over the fire and let it heat up. He explained that in refining silver, one needed to hold the silver in the middle of the fire where the flames were hottest as to burn away all the impurities. The woman thought about God holding us in such a hot spot and then she thought again about the verse that says: "He sits as a refiner and purifier of silver." She watched as sweat poured from his brow due to the intensity of the heat from the fire he sat so close to. She asked the silversmith if it was true that he had to sit there in front of the fire the whole time the silver was being refined.

The man answered that yes, he not only had to sit there holding the silver, but he had to keep his eyes on the silver the entire time it was in the fire. If the silver was left a moment too long in the flames, it would be destroyed.

The woman was silent for a moment. Then she asked the silversmith, "How do you know when the silver is fully refined?"

He smiled at her and answered, "Oh, that's easy - when I see my image in it."

If today you are feeling the heat of the fire, remember that God has His eye on you and will keep watching you until He sees His image in you.

This was the motivation I needed…to get away from focusing on me and how I felt and focus on what to do about the people I cared about. I did have to close the business, but before I did, I made arrangements through other local establishments and yes, even competitors, to employ most of my staff.

It's not who you see in the mirror, but who you are looking for.

Listen Up

To help assess the motives of someone, you need to be a good listener. Many times, reflective listening is a very useful tool. To do a good job of reflective listening, you don't just repeat what the speaker is saying, you should re-word his statement so that he not only thinks you understand the context of what he is saying, but also the feelings behind it.

To be an effective listener, you don't have to feel his feelings, or agree with his point of view; however, you do need to let him understand that you are aware of his feelings on the matter.

A good listener doesn't assume he knows what the speaker is feeling, but probes the speaker to find out if he is following on the right track. The best way is simply by asking, i.e. "Did you feel embarrassed?", "Did you feel a sense of control?" etc. Ask about feelings, because feelings are better indicators of what's going on in a person's life. What people think is what they use for preparation in a decision. How they feel is where those thoughts are directed for those decisions.

People are less afraid to bare their soul to someone they are completely comfortable with. The closer you are to their comfort zone, the more accurate the dialogue. If you are not on the right track, the speaker will not be threatened or uncomfortable in correcting you, provided your questions are in a non-invasive approach.

Sometimes it's good to use statements like "let me make sure I understand what you're telling me…"; or "are you telling me that…" Then see if you have a correct interpretation by reiterating the statement in your own words.

Your job as a listener is to bring out their feelings on a subject they might rather choose to repress. You shouldn't try to tell them how to feel or try to protect them from their feelings. Repressed feelings will always eventually surface—usually in an inappropriate manner.

As a husband, I have a need to fix things. I can fix almost anything. When my wife has a problem, my natural reaction is to fix it. It doesn't matter if it's tangible or emotional… I want to fix it. I find on the emotional side she doesn't necessarily need a "fix", she wants an audience. We shouldn't try to fix every one's problems. As a person, everyone has a right to their own feelings. It may be beneficial for you to help them determine their origin, classify their emotions, and help them catalog them for future use, but they have a right and responsibility to deal with them.

Confidence in expressing one's feelings will break down emotional facades, and that's what you're after as a listener; their underlying feelings—what motivates them—the agenda behind their opinion.

Occasionally, you'll find the subject at hand is itself a barricade to the real problem.

Some times, people talk about less significant subjects to "test the waters" before they feel comfortable with pouring their more sensitive troubles on you.

By understanding their emotional side, it will help you to be able to determine how you should deal with their personality.

Communication

Communication is not just transference of information. It is passing on of ideas that will in almost all cases be perceived with differing emotional impact. Hopefully, the impact sent is similarly received. When a motivational speaker, for example, uses a parable to illustrate a point, he knows what emotional impact he is trying to create. The impact is as different as the personalities listening to him, because the way each person emotionally adapts the communication to his or her circumstances determines the effectiveness of the thought. The *fuzzy logic* of this is that he wants to cause the highest impact to the most people possible.

If you're going to communicate effectively, you need to cut through all the unnecessary jargon and facades, and deal directly with their emotions. Logic, facts and figures can be used to get them to understand the details and reasons. Decisions, though they may be cognitively logical in formulation and filtration, are not decisions until an emotional commitment propels it. The stronger the emotion, the stronger the commitment.

When I had employees that tell me they forgot where they left something, I would say "Let me see your keys, I need to prove a point." Confused, they would hand me their keys and I would walk over to a table and very loudly and forcefully slam their keys on the table. Then I would walk back and gently say to them "When I ask you three weeks from now where I put your keys, will you remember?" The answer would inevitably be "Absolutely, how can I *not* remember that?" Then I would explain that the point I wanted to make was that when I suddenly out of the blue seemed highly emotional, their reaction was also emotional and made a much deeper impact on their memory than if I had just set the keys on a table. My suggestion to them then would be that the next time they put something down that they had forgotten before, to imagine that it explodes and left a big mark on the place they left it. That way, the emotional impact would make it much easier for them to remember. With practice, life can be more positive and enjoyable through being more emotionally directed, instead of a compilation of rote acts.

If you want someone to take what you say seriously, you must make sure they perceive it emotionally, and the best way to do that is to present it emotionally. Assuming you are always looking for win/win situations, your emotions should always be uplifting, and honorable.

If you want to take what *you* think you should do to a higher level, you should get more emotional about what you want. Communicate emotionally to yourself.

You should be your best listener.

Impact on Children

Many of the new ideas about dealing with children as far as behavior development goes, is that you separate behavior from the child as a person. I can understand this to an extent. I understand that as a parent you should love your children in spite of their faults. An approach to negative behavior is to say that you are disappointed in their behavior but still love them as a person. A major point pushed is that their behavior does not dictate whether or not they are loved, needed, deserving of protection or valued as a person. Also, good behavior deserves reward and or appreciation, like a pat on the back or a kind word, or tangible rewards. This sounds all good and fine, and I choose not to disagree with the reward part for good behavior; however, this theory doesn't go far enough. As you reward a child for good behavior, you also add emotional impact to his understanding of what he just did.

As a child learns that good behavior produces rewards either accompanied by affection or as just the affection itself, he is also able to deduce that bad behavior deprives him of such affection or valued attention, or at least it should. He basically has no choice but to believe affection is a result of behavior. Catching someone in the act of doing something right and praising them for it is a win/win situation for everyone—even if you have to create the situation. This is not just for children. There have been several times that I have purposefully made it nearly impossible for one of my employees to foul up a request of mine for the sole purpose of being able to commend them on a job well done. The more situations that occur, the more self-esteem is built, and the more emotion is assigned to doing the *right* thing for the person who does the praising. Through this practice you will see that emotion produces behavior.

If you agree that you cannot separate a person from his behavior because emotion causes behavior, *and* that how you react to a person's behavior is also an emotional response, then we can effectively work on emotion to control behavior.

It all comes back to what is important. If it is important that your child does a particular chore for example, he may think it is more important to play or even do something to avoid that chore. This is where your opportunity comes to convince your child it is more important to understand and appease you than to stand on what *he* had valued as important at the time. You must be certain that he understands and anticipates your emotions, because all his life he has placed significance in your approval. Don't shirk your responsibility. The more self-esteem that is created, the stronger the emotional bond is to its initiator. It is of utmost importance that once he understands and submits, that you immediately give your approval by an affectionate hug, and/or a kind affirmation such as "thank you for taking care of that for me, you made me very happy". The point is to get him to feel good about the encounter, and if he feels good about the encounter, it is also important to point out the good feeling he is having for doing a good job. This allows him to be proud of himself. This confirms that even though he didn't get his way, there is an upside that he can place value on. If you just let this theory go, there is a good possibility he will seek attention through negative behavior. He's trying to fill the voids in his P.L.A.C.E. in life. That particular route can be curbed.

Another important part is that you recognize that he is #1 in his life and will always have a "what's in it for me" agenda that he has to contend with. If you have the opportunity to point out the importance of how his behavior will affect him personally, you have two things going for you… value placement for him and anticipated acknowledgement from you.

Responsibilities

There are probably multitudes of things you are responsible for in the course of your daily life. In being responsible, you not only need to be accountable, but need to have authority to have input or at least some control to exercise your responsibilities. A lot of us don't want as much responsibility as we have, and sometimes find ways to disburse it. Delegation is a good relief if it is available. Not everyone can overcome all obstacles, but all too often we find ourselves compromising our sense of accountability and placing blame to avoid embarrassment or guilt.

Remember, one still has to tell himself he's okay. So, what's the answer when things go awry? Ask yourself "Am I satisfied that I did all I can do?" Or; "Am I satisfied that I did enough?" Only you can give that answer. You're the one who has to live with your results, but, on the other hand, you need to realize that your best *is* good enough. Do you have warm fuzzies after it's over?

What you don't want to do is come up with excuses of why things or people or circumstances aren't falling into place, or tell yourself you're incompetent and become a martyr of your environment. Especially when you do the latter, you don't really blame yourself, because you have to tell yourself that you're still okay. As a result, in the back of your mind, you blame society for not allowing you to be anything else. Not good... That fosters retribution.

What you should be after is the calm, "Peace like a river" feeling of having done your part and be able to wash your hands of the burdens that accompany an unfulfilled, or partial attempt. Of course, there will be times where you didn't do all you could, and you have to live with the consequences.

Look, there are plenty of outer influences that can beat you down, even to the point that you may be just a shell of the person you want to be. If you are always looking back, you'll never see what's in front of you, and there are always stumbling blocks along the way. It would be better to see what's coming and step around, rather than continuously pick yourself up after each stumble. Be aware that each fall does take a toll on your ego and influences your outlook. Your past is to learn from, not to be traumatized by. If you want your influences to come from positive results building upon each previous success, you need to be willing to go the extra mile once in a while to make it happen. Your results from doing a little extra will build you into a more confident and responsible person. Your warm fuzzies will accelerate, become more satisfying, and promote more of the same.

How Do I Win?

Because we are all self-centered beings that are influenced by other self-centered beings, how can we possibly succeed? Why were we created this way? Was it that we evolved from a need for survival, or did our Creator have something else in mind?

This makes me think of the atheistic or scientific question as to whether or not God is so powerful that he would be able to create a rock so big that he couldn't lift it. There are two problems with that premise. One would be that the questioner would be limiting the Creator to an entity that would require of him to be in a form that would need to lift something to be able to prove it. Would the questioner have the authority to place such limits on the Creator in order to get his question answered? The second problem, also pertaining to authority, would be that, if God had chosen to place limits on himself; would the questioner allow God's choice to limit Himself be a premise available for consideration.

Okay, if God so loves us, then, why would he put limits on himself and allow bad things to happen to us? How about this for an answer... Free will.

He gives us the ability to choose. It's that simple. If we were not given the ability to choose, we would be nothing more than mind numbed robots. Being forced to love is not love. Even in the Garden of Eden, the choice was given regarding forbidden fruit. God has apparently assigned a few laws and principles. One of the harshest of them would be that, "with choices, come consequences". We will continue to live with the results of our choices. Some consequences have positive implications, and others, not so much. Some end in death and destruction. Why is it so hard? We all fall short of the glory.

Until the end of the age, we will be unable to act without considering "What's in it for me?" Could it be that in this 'It's all about me' world we should emulate the one who showed us 'it's all about you'? To me, this brings an enlightenment of the biblical reference of everyone being born in sin. If God is all about giving, and we're all about taking, which, in itself, takes us out of fellowship with God, then that pretty much sums it up. But all is not lost. No, this is not where I tell you how to reconcile with God, but you and everyone you come in contact with can benefit from *you* properly using that knowledge. Why love thy neighbor *as thyself* and not *as thy other neighbor*? Apparently, He already figured out this "self" thing for us.

Here's where the full extent of "warm fuzzy logic" comes into play...

Act as if you're ***not*** number one. Calendar how you will help someone else. Assume that everyone you come into contact with has a "wellbeing" status that's at least as important as yours. When you're focused on helping someone else, you both benefit. You have less time to worry about your own problems. You're warm fuzzies are more intense and longer lasting. The more you act on *not* being number one, the more rewards you get from it. Yes, it can actually become a habit that you will seek to fulfill because of the positive results. Surround yourself with people that will positively influence you. Remember everyone influences you in some way. You obviously influence others that you come in contact with in one way or another. Consider the ways in which you can choose to influence them. Since you're taking time to think about other's needs, you also have time to find their motivations. Because you enjoy being acknowledged and complimented, take the first step in making someone else smile.

Look for someone doing something right and praise them for it. Not everyone is blessed with the opportunity to affect the people *you* come in contact with. These people need you. Gratitude is the best attitude.

Originally, I ended this particular chapter with those last two thoughts (These people need you. Gratitude is the best attitude.). I was convinced that I had finished this book, editing and all. Recently, I was driving home and was thinking about the ending of this chapter. A thought kept coming back to me. "Your message here isn't strong enough, it won't reach enough people." I kept telling myself I was finished and ready for print, but the thought still kept coming back, and I couldn't figure out why. As I continued to drive, a story was revealed to me, and I found myself fighting the details as they came to me because it was causing my eyes to well up as I was sensing the outcome of the story.

It took place in the early 1900's. A gentleman was coming out of a grocery store and saw a young lady who seemed to be homeless and a bit sickly. He took it upon himself to go over to her and offer a dollar to help the troubled lady. He struck up a conversation and found that she was indeed homeless. During the conversation she told him that she had a dream the previous night that was stronger than any she'd had before; more like a premonition. She said she heard a voice from God saying, "I will send someone to you to comfort you and resolve your problems." She followed with "God always keeps his promises." He said how do you know he promised? Her reply was, "If he spoke it, then that made it a promise."

He was intrigued by her reasoning and enjoying her conversation. Thinking she does look in need, and could probably use a good meal, he asked her if she would like to come to his house for dinner. She accepted and during the dinner, he thought it would be okay to allow her to spend a few days at his house until this person, of which she spoke, and was so adamantly convinced would show up. She didn't want to impose, but he assured her there was no difficulty on his part, and someday he'd like to meet this person.

Days turned into months, but he didn't mind her company, and was growing fond of nurturing her back to health, though at times he wondered about her "promise from God".

One day, she became very ill and couldn't get out of bed. She was losing color as her skin was becoming pale. She could hardly speak and when she did, it could only be in a whisper.

Kneeling at her bedside, he could see that she was going fast. He thought back to the promise. With tears in his eyes, knowing that he was losing a friend, almost in distain, he demanded, "What about the promise from God to bring someone to comfort you and resolve your problems? You said he always keeps his promises."

She slowly turned her head to him and whispered, "I had another dream last night. He spoke to me again. He said today is the day He will bring me home to Him. He said He always keeps his promises. Thank you. You were the promise he spoke of." At that moment her eyes closed, and his heart opened to the journey that awaited them both.

    Take a journey.
    You may be someone's answer.

NOT! Lost in Space

As a final exercise, let's touch on multiple dimensions for just a bit. You may have learned about parts of this in algebra, and furthered your application if you took geometry. Start with no dimensions. How do you define non-dimensional? A point on a line that you've drawn on a piece of paper. The point itself has no width or height; it's just something specific to relate to. The line itself that you drew it on is one-dimensional. It has width… a beginning and an end. The paper that you drew it on has width

and height, making it two-dimensional. You personally, having width, height, and depth, are a three-dimensional being, and can place the point on any part of the line which *you* drew. Don't stop with dimensions. Think of the point on the line on the paper as the place to assign a time at which you drew it. Time is the fourth dimension and placement on the timeline is the next in the series of dimensions. If any of these dimensions were not a factor, you would never be able to assign a time to the point you drew.
And here's my point.

When I first described the point on the line, I showed the requirements to go to each level. When you get to the fourth dimension, we were talking about the timing that you placed a point on a line that *you* created. You could have placed that point anywhere on the line because you are the higher source and have the choice of doing so. You also created the line. You have control over it. It did not create you. You chose its beginning and end. You are the higher power of the lower dimensions.

Where is *your* point on life's timeline? Who placed you there? You're there for a reason (of some one's choosing). Put value in your life. If you continue to follow the dimensional theory to higher dimensions, someone will have control over the timeline itself. For me, the one in control is God. A higher power than you chose your point on the timeline. You're right here, right now for a reason that The Almighty has chosen for you. **Make it count.**

When it's all said and done, all we have of any real value are memories. When you set your soul on fire, you emblaze dreams into memories. Build something that's worth being burned into your memories.

I don't have all the answers, but maybe along the way, I've re-framed the questions in a way that's different enough to help you come up with some of your own answers.

Don't just think about it. It takes ***effort*** on your part to make the rest of your life the best of your life.

No one expects you to walk on water, but for God's sake, go get your feet wet!

Made in the USA
Middletown, DE
04 May 2022